Colours
for the Soul

PAM RHODES has presented *Songs of Praise*,
the world's number-one religious television
programme, since 1987. Prior to that she was
a journalist and a television news presenter.
She is also a successful novelist.

Colours
for the Soul

PAM RHODES

A LION BOOK

A Lion Book
an imprint of
Lion Hudson plc
Mayfield House, 256 Banbury Road,
Oxford OX2 7DH, England
www.lionhudson.com
ISBN 0 7459 5110 4

First hardback edition 2002
First paperback edition 2004
10 9 8 7 6 5 4 3 2 1

A catalogue record for this book is available
from the British Library

Typeset in 11/16 Humanist 521
Printed and bound in China

Contents

Introduction

Sometimes words fail you. Sometimes thoughts are too confused, obstacles too terrifying, courage too weak, energy too low or emotions too raw for you to put into words how you feel, what you need or what you would like others to know.

At times like that, this book is for you. And at other times too, when a touch of down-to-earth humour can bring a welcome smile to your face, you'll find something within these covers to put daily life into perspective. All these quotes come from people who've been exactly where you are now – whether in fact they were living 2,000 years ago, or very much in the

present day. And their reaction,
pragmatism and sense of fun,
encapsulated in words, are
likely to be just what you
need to find comfort,
encouragement and
common sense to face
your own troubles today.
So dip in and discover which
colour speaks to you. May you find
the inspiration you need to help you
through our modern-day maze of love,
loss, fear and confusion. And may it bring you
the peace and fulfilment for which you long.

Red
for
relationships

… when you've
found, lost or
yearned for love

Love is a many-splendoured thing

Oh, life is a glorious cycle of song,
    a medley of extemporanea!
And love is a thing that can never go wrong –
    and I am Marie of Rumania!

Dorothy Parker

When love is not madness, it is not love.

Pedro Calderon de la Barca

He turns not back who
is bound to a star.

Leonardo da Vinci

We are each of us angels with only one wing.
And we can fly only by embracing each other.

Luciano de Crescenzo

Having a dream isn't stupid. It's not having a dream that's stupid.

Anon

I am seeking, I am striving, I am in it with all my heart.

Vincent van Gogh

In order to have great happiness, you have to have great pain and unhappiness – otherwise how would you know when you were happy?

Leslie Caron

If you have to be in a soup opera, try not to get the worst role.

Boy George

If only one could tell true love from false love as one can tell mushrooms from toadstools.

Katherine Mansfield

Love is a fire – but whether it's going to warm your hearth or burn down your house, you can never tell.

Joan Crawford

He loves me...

Follow your bliss.

Joseph Campbell

There are no rules.
Just follow your heart.

Robin Williams

Oh, the comfort, the inexpressible comfort
   of feeling safe with a person;
having neither to weigh thoughts nor measure words,
   but to pour them all out just as they are,
     chaff and grain together,
   knowing that a faithful hand will take and sift them,
     keep what is worth keeping,
and then, with the breath of kindness,
   blow the rest away.

George Eliot

Who so loves believes the impossible.

Elizabeth Barrett Browning

Nobody is perfect – until
you fall in love with them.

Anon

What counts in making a happy marriage
is not so much how compatible you are,
but how you deal with incompatibility.

George Levinger

Throw your heart out in front of
you – and run ahead to catch it.

Arab proverb

I love you not only for what
you have made of yourself, but
for what you are making of me.

Ray Croft

Love teaches even asses to dance.

French proverb

The day he moved out was terrible –
that evening she went through hell.
His absence wasn't a problem,
but the corkscrew had gone as well.

Wendy Cope

What do you do when the
only person who can make
you stop crying is the person
who made you cry?

Anon

He
loves
me
not...

Fool me once,
shame on you:
fool me twice,
shame on me.

Chinese proverb

With the catching
ends the pleasure
of the chase.

Abraham Lincoln

One man –
two loves.
No good ever
comes of that.

Euripides

Grumbling is the death of love.

Marlene Dietrich

*I have the true feeling of myself only
when I am unbearably unhappy.*

Franz Kafka

*I am not responsible for your happiness,
any more than you are responsible for mine.*

Anon

*Don't cry over anyone
who won't cry over you.*

Anon

*What shall a woman do with her ego,
faced with the choice that it go – or he go?*

Alma Denny

*Don't compromise yourself.
You are all you've got.*

Janis Joplin

*Kindness is in our power,
even when fondness is not.*

Samuel Johnson

Forgiveness is the sweetest revenge.

Isaac Friedmann

*Letting people be OK
without us is how we get
to be OK without them.*

Merrit Malloy

*Lady, lady, should you meet
one whose ways are all discreet,
one who murmurs that his wife
is the lodestar of his life,
one who keeps assuring you
that he never was untrue,
never loved another one…
lady, lady, better run!*

Dorothy Parker

*To err is human,
to forgive divine.*

Alexander Pope

*Whoever lies down with
dogs shall rise up with fleas.*

Anon

*Somebody's boring
me. I think it's me.*

Dylan Thomas

*The really happy person is one who
can enjoy the scenery on a detour.*

Anon

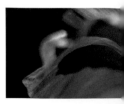

Having found it, don't lose it

Marriage is not just spiritual communion and passionate embraces; marriage is also three meals a day, sharing the workload and remembering to carry out the trash.

Dr Joyce Brothers

Remember always that you have not only the right to be an individual, you have an obligation to be one.

Eleanor Roosevelt

When everything has to be right, something isn't.

Stanislaw Lec

If you want to be listened to, you should put in time listening.

Marge Piercy

Once a woman has forgiven a man, she must not reheat his sins for breakfast.

Marlene Dietrich

Why destroy your present happiness by a distant
misery, which may never come at all?
For every substantial grief has twenty
shadows and most of the shadows
are of your own making.

Sydney Smith

An archaeologist is the best
husband any woman can have:
the older she gets, the more
interested he is in her.

Agatha Christie

Be like a postage stamp – stick
to one thing until you get there.

Josh Billings

Remember that sometimes
silence is the best answer.

Anon

Longing for love

I'm in love with the potential
of miracles. For me, the safest
place is out on a limb.

Shirley MacLaine

Faint heart never won fair lady.

Miguel de Cervantes

Don't leave before
the miracle
happens!

Anon

A man can be short
and dumpy and
getting bald, but if
he has fire, women
will like him.

Mae West

I'm not there yet – but
I'm closer than I was yesterday.

Anon

If we resist our
passions, it is more
from their weakness
than from our strength.

François de la Rochefoucauld

A smooth sea never made a skilful mariner.

English proverb

When a man does not know
what harbour he is making for,
no wind is the right wind.

Marcus Annaeus Seneca

Come here and give me a cuddle,
   sit on my lap and give me a hug,
while we are both still enjoying
   this mysterious whirling planet.
And if you find me fat, you find me
   also easy to find, very easy to find.

Joyce la Verne

What a lovely surprise to discover
how un-lonely being alone can be.

Anon

Flops are a part of life's menu,
and I've never been a girl to miss
out on any of the courses.

Rosalind Russell

None but the brave deserves the fair.

John Dryden

Anyone who's a great kisser
I'm always interested in!

Cher

We spend our time searching for
security, and hate it when we get it.

John Steinbeck

Friends are the family we choose for ourselves

It's the friends
you can call up at
4 a.m. that matter.

Marlene Dietrich

'Stay' is a charming word
in a friend's vocabulary.

Louisa May Alcott

Friendship is love
without his wings!

Lord Byron

There is no physician
like a true friend.

Anon

The feeling of friendship is like
that of being comfortably filled
with roast beef; love, like being
enlivened with champagne.

Samuel Johnson

Chance makes our parents,
but choice makes our friends.

Jacques Delille

If you want an accounting of
your worth, count your friends.

Merry Browne

If you don't stand for something,
you'll fall for anything.

Michael Evans

There is nothing we like to see so much as the gleam of pleasure in a person's eye when he feels that we have sympathised with him, understood him, interested ourselves in his welfare. At these moments something fine and spiritual passes between two friends. These moments are the moments worth living for.

Don Marquis

You can always tell a real friend: when you've made a fool of yourself, he doesn't feel you've done a permanent job.

Laurence J. Peter

The bird, a nest; the spider, a web; man, friendship.

William Blake

The most beautiful discovery true friends make is that they can grow separately without growing apart.

Elizabeth Foley

A loyal friend laughs at your jokes when they're not so good, and sympathises with your problems when they're not so bad.

Arnold H. Glasgow

*I like a friend who will stand by me,
not only when I am in the right, but
when I am a little in the wrong.*
Sir Walter Scott

*Greater love hath no man
than this, that a man lay
down his life for his friends.*
John's Gospel

*Yes'm, old friends is always best,
'less you can catch a new one that's
fit to make an old one out of.*
Sarah Orne Jewett

*Silences make the real
conversations between friends.*
Margaret Lee Runbeck

*Two people, yes, two lasting friends.
    The giving comes, the taking ends.
There is no measure for such things.
    For this all nature slows and sings.*
Elizabeth Jennings

*My true friends have always
given me that supreme proof
of devotion: a spontaneous
aversion for the man I loved.*
Colette

*There's nothing worth the wear of winning,
but laughter and the love of friends.*
Hillaire Belloc

Don't judge others by their relatives

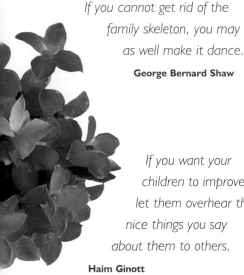

If you cannot get rid of the family skeleton, you may as well make it dance.

George Bernard Shaw

If you want your children to improve, let them overhear the nice things you say about them to others.

Haim Ginott

Make happy those who are near, and those who are far will come.

Chinese proverb

One would be in less danger from the wiles of the stranger if one's own kin and kith were more fun to be with.

Ogden Nash

Never grow a wishbone, daughter, where your backbone ought to be.

Clementine Paddleford

I was not a classic mother
— but my kids were never
palmed off to boarding school.
So I didn't bake cookies.
You can buy cookies
— but you can't buy love.

Raquel Welsh

Those that will have a perfect
brother must resign themselves
to remaining brotherless.

Italian proverb

Children aren't happy with nothing to ignore,
and that's what parents were created for.

Ogden Nash

Did I conceive a child?
Or child, by forming,
did you conceive a mother?

Carol Van Klompenburg

The history of humanity is not the history
of its wars, but the history of its households.

John Ruskin

To love others, you must first love yourself

If you must love your neighbour
as yourself, it is at least as fair to
love yourself as your neighbour.

Nicolas de Chamfort

It is not the eyes of
others that I am wary
of, but my own.

Noel Coward

This above all: to thine own self be true.

William Shakespeare

I always thought I should
be treated like a star.

Madonna

If there are 200 people
in a room and one of
them doesn't like me,
I've got to get out.

Marlon Brando

I am somebody. I am me.
I like being me. And I need
nobody to make me somebody.

Louis l'Amour

Take the time to come
home to yourself every day.

Robin Casarjean

It is better to be hated for what you
are than loved for what you are not.

Andre Gide

There is nothing wrong with
making mistakes. Just don't
respond with encores.

Anon

I feel there are two people
inside me – me and my intuition.
If I go against her, she'll screw
me every time, and if I follow
her, we get along quite nicely.

Kim Basinger

Every man must get to
heaven his own way.

Frederick the Great

I go by instinct – I don't
worry about experience.

Barbra Streisand

And in the end, the love you take
is equal to the love you make.

Paul McCartney

Life only demands from you
the strength you possess.

Dag Hammarskjold

We're all in this together... alone.

Lily Tomlin

If a man hasn't discovered
something that he will
die for, he isn't fit to live.

Martin Luther King, Jr

A woman is like a tea bag – you never know
her strength until you drop her in hot water.

Nancy Reagan

Blue
for
healing

… when you long for
comfort and courage
to cope with grief,
pain or uncertainty

What hurts

We must learn from
life how to suffer it.

French proverb

The biggest thing in
today's sorrow is the
memory of yesterday's joy.

Kahlil Gibran

Never to suffer would have been
never to have been blessed.

Edgar Allan Poe

Holding on to anger is
like grasping a hot coal
with the intent of throwing
it at someone else — you are
the one who gets burned.

The Buddha

Despair is the price one pays for
setting oneself an impossible aim.

Graham Greene

Perhaps some day it will be
pleasant to remember even this.

Virgil

Unfortunately, sometimes people
don't hear you until you scream.

Stefanie Powers

Were women meant to do
everything — work and have babies?

Candice Bergen

Being unwanted, unloved, uncared
for, forgotten by everybody — I think
that is a much greater hunger, a
much greater poverty, than the
person who has nothing to eat...
We must find each other.

Mother Teresa

Worry often gives a small
thing a big shadow.

Swedish proverb

Fear makes the wolf
bigger than it is.

German proverb

Hope is grief's best music.

Anon

Oh Lord, thou givest us everything,
at the price of an effort.
Leonardo da Vinci

That money talks, I won't deny.
I heard it once. It said, 'Goodbye.'
Richard Armour

Your pain is the breaking of the shell
that encloses your understanding.
Kahlil Gibran

I'm a little wounded,
but I am not slain.
I will lay me down to bleed a while.
Then I'll rise and fight again.
John Dryden

I have lost friends, some by
death... others through sheer
inability to cross the street.
Virginia Woolf

The gem cannot be polished
without friction, nor man
perfected without trials.
Confucius

We should not let our fears hold us back from pursuing our hopes.
John F. Kennedy

There are worse things than having behaved foolishly in public. There are worse things than these miniature betrayals committed or endured or suspected; there are worse things than not being able to sleep for thinking about them. It is 5 a.m. All the worse things come stalking in and stand icily about the bed looking worse and worse and worse.

Fleur Adcock

Every path has its puddle.

English proverb

We are more often frightened than hurt – and we suffer more from imagination than from reality.

Marcus Annaeus Seneca

He never knew when he was whipped... so he never was.

Louis l'Amour

God will not look you over for medals, degrees or diplomas, but for scars.

Anon

*Don't let a kick in the ass
stop you. It's how you cope
that says what you are.*

George Cukor

*The difficulties of life
are intended to make
us better, not bitter.*

Anon

*Inside of a ring or out, ain't
nothing wrong with going down.
It's staying down that's wrong.*

Muhammad Ali

*The smartest thing I ever
said was, 'Help me.'*

Anon

Whenever you fall, pick something up.

Oswald Avery

Groan and forget it.

Jessamyn West

Fear – the best way out is through.

Helen Keller

*You are sad now, but I shall
see you again, and your hearts
will be full of joy, and that joy
no one shall take from you.*

John's Gospel

I will not forget you! See, I have engraved you on the palms of my hands.

Book of Isaiah

What helps

Perhaps I am stronger than I think.

Thomas Merton

What you are afraid to do is a clear indicator of the next thing you need to do.

Anon

Doubt whom you will, but never yourself.

Christian Bovée

I wept because I had no shoes – until I saw a man who had no feet.

Ancient Persian saying

From a distance, it is something
– and nearby, it is nothing.
Jean de la Fontaine

Your real security is yourself. You
know you can do it, and they can't
ever take that away from you.
Mae West

Hold your head high, stick your
chest out. You can make it.
It gets dark sometimes, but
morning comes. Keep hope alive.
Jesse Jackson

Your faith has made you
well. Go in peace, and be
healed of your trouble.
Mark's Gospel

Start by doing what's
necessary, then what's
possible, and suddenly you
are doing the impossible.
St Francis of Assisi

The greater the obstacle, the more glory in overcoming it.

Jean Baptiste Poquelin Molière

All I would tell people is to hold on to what was individual about themselves, not to allow their ambition for success to cause them to try to imitate the success of others. You've got to find it on your own terms.

Harrison Ford

Strength does not come from winning. Your struggles develop your strengths. When you go through hardships and decide not to surrender, that is strength.

Arnold Schwarzenegger

Let me win, but if I cannot win, let me be brave in the attempt.

Motto of the Special Olympics

Today I bent the truth to be kind, and I have no regret, for I am far surer of what is kind than I am of what is true.

Robert Brault

Always forgive your enemies; nothing annoys them so much.

Oscar Wilde

Better bend than break.

Scottish proverb

I walk firmer and more secure up hill than down.

Michel de Montaigne

He is lifeless that is faultless.

English proverb

When you dig another out
of their troubles, you find
a place to bury your own.

Anon

Cast thy burden upon the Lord,
and he shall sustain thee.

Book of Psalms

To lose is to learn.

Anon

You have striven so hard, and so long,
to compel life. Can't you now slowly
change, and let life slowly drift into
you… let the invisible life steal into
you and slowly possess you?

D.H. Lawrence

If you have no will to change it,
you have no right to criticise it.

Anon

For peace of mind, resign as
general manager of the universe.

Anon

Don't be discouraged. It
is often the last key in the
bunch that opens the lock.

Anon

If we could read the secret history of our enemies, we would find in each man's life a sorrow and a suffering enough to disarm all hostility.

Henry Wadsworth Longfellow

When things go wrong, don't go with them.

Anon

Let go, let God.

Anon

Once we truly know that life is difficult – once we truly understand and accept it – then life is no longer difficult. Because once it is accepted, the fact that life is difficult no longer matters.

M. Scott Peck

God has not given you a spirit
of fear, but of power and love.

Paul's second letter to Timothy

Pain is never permanent.

Teresa of Avila

In this world there are
only two tragedies.
One is not getting
what one wants, and
the other is getting it.

Oscar Wilde

What
we
need
to
know

We have fought this
fight as long, and
as well, as we know
how. We have been
defeated... there is
now but one course
to pursue. We must
accept the situation.

Robert E. Lee

Do what you can, with what
you have, where you are.

Theodore Roosevelt

When a heart is
broken, God takes care
of all the little pieces.

Anon

No one can
make you feel
inferior without
your consent.

Eleanor Roosevelt

If at first you don't
succeed, you're
running about average.

M.H. Alderson

What lies in our power to do,
it lies in our power not to do.

Aristotle

To dream of the person
you would like to be is to
waste the person you are.

Anon

The fault, dear Brutus, is not
in our stars, but in ourselves.

William Shakespeare

Never bend your head. Hold it high.
Look the world straight in the eye.

Helen Keller

Sorrow is a fruit. God does not allow it to grow on a branch that is too weak to bear it.

Victor Hugo

If you judge people, you have no time to love them.

Mother Teresa

If you have one eye on yesterday, and one eye on tomorrow, you're going to be cock-eyed today.

Anon

A flower falls even though we love it. A weed grows even though we don't.

Dogen Sangha

He who fears something gives it power over him.

Moorish proverb

Any concern too small to be turned into a prayer is too small to be made into a burden.

Corrie ten Boom

The door of opportunity won't
open unless you do some pushing.

Anon

Keep doing what you're doing and
you'll keep getting what you're getting.

Anon

The way I see it – if you want the
rainbow, you gotta put up with the rain.

Dolly Parton

Some people walk in the
rain. Others just get wet.

Roger Miller

You can't have
everything. Where
would you put it?

Ann Landers

Failure is only an opportunity to
begin again more intelligently.

Henry Ford

For so must it be, and
help me to do my part.

A Tibetan master

Yellow for encouragement

… reassurance that
you have all you need
within and around you
to face whatever
comes your way

Happiness is...

To laugh often and much;
to win the respect of intelligent people,
    and the affection of children;
to earn the appreciation of honest critics,
    and endure the betrayal of false friends;
to appreciate beauty;
to find the best in others;
to leave the world a bit better,
  whether by a healthy child, a garden patch
    or a redeemed social condition;
to know that even one life has breathed
    easier because you lived.
This is to have succeeded.

Ralph Waldo Emerson

Happiness is when what
you think, what you say and
what you do are in harmony.

Mahatma Gandhi

Yes, there is a nirvana: it is in leading your sheep to a green pasture, and in putting your child to sleep, and in writing the last line of your poem.

Kahlil Gibran

Earth's crammed with heaven.

Elizabeth Barrett Browning

He did it with all his heart, and prospered.

Book of Chronicles

Most of us miss out on life's big prizes. The Pullitzer. The Nobel. Oscars. Tonys. Emmys. But we're all eligible for life's small pleasures. A pat on the back. A kiss behind the ear. A four-pound bass. A full moon. An empty parking space. A crackling fire. A great meal. A glorious sunset. Hot soup. Cold beer. Don't fret about copping life's great awards. Enjoy its tiny delights. There are plenty for all of us.

United Technologies Corporation
advertisement

*Those who bring sunshine
to the lives of others cannot
keep it from themselves.*
James M. Barrie

*Give me a man who
sings at his work.*
Thomas Carlyle

*There are three ingredients
in the good life – learning,
earning and yearning.*
Christopher Morely

*This is true joy of life – being used for
a purpose that is recognised by yourself
as a mighty one – instead of being a
feverish, selfish little clod of ailments and
grievances, complaining that the world
will not devote itself to making you happy.*
George Bernard Shaw

To be without some of the things you want
is an indispensable part of happiness.
Success is getting what you want;
happiness is wanting what you get.

Anon

There is great happiness in not wanting,
in not being somewhere,
in not going somewhere.

J. Krishnamurti

The sense of existence is the greatest happiness.

Benjamin Disraeli

Think of all the beauty that's still left
in and around you and be happy!

Anne Frank

He is the happiest, be he king or
peasant, who finds peace in his home.

Johann Wolfgang von Goethe

My advice to you is not to enquire why or whither, but just enjoy your ice cream while it's on your plate.

Thornton Wilder

We are all in the gutter, but some of us are looking at the stars.

Oscar Wilde

Reasons to be cheerful

Thank God every morning when you get up that you have something to do that day which must be done, whether you like it or not.

Charles Kingsley

You will never enjoy the world aright till the sea itself floweth in your veins, till you are clothed with the heavens and crowned with the stars.

Thomas Traherne

Nine requisites for contented living:
health enough to make work a pleasure;
wealth enough to support your needs;
strength to battle with difficulties and overcome them;
grace enough to confess your sins and forsake them;
patience enough to toil until some good is accomplished;
charity enough to see some good in your neighbour;
love enough to move you to be useful and
helpful to others;
faith enough to make real the things of God;
hope enough to remove all anxious fears
concerning the future.

Johann Wolfgang von Goethe

What a wonderful life I've had!
I only wish I'd realised it sooner.

Colette

I got the blues thinking of the
future, so I left off and made
some marmalade. It's amazing
how it cheers one up to shred
oranges and scrub the floor.

D.H. Lawrence

Rule number one is don't sweat the small stuff.
Rule number two is it's all small stuff.

Robert Eliot

I finally figured out the only
reason to be alive is to enjoy it.

Rita Mae Brown

To make the world a friendly place,
one must show it a friendly face.

James Whitcomb Riley

It was only a sunny smile,
and little it cost in the giving.
But like morning light, it scattered the night,
and made the day worth living.

Anon

One who smiles rather than
rages is always the stronger.

Japanese saying

With the rising of the sun, think of your life as just begun.

Anon

This is the day the Lord has made;
let us rejoice and be glad in it.

Book of Psalms

Worry is a futile thing;
it's somewhat like a rocking chair:
although it keeps you occupied,
it doesn't get you anywhere.

Anon

I am not happy, I'm cheerful. There's a difference. A
happy woman has no cares at all. A cheerful woman
has cares, but has learned how to deal with them.

Beverly Sills

Count your blessings

I asked for riches that I might be happy;
I was given poverty that I might be wise.

I asked for all things that I might enjoy life;
I was given life that I might enjoy all things.

I was given nothing that I asked for;
but everything that I had hoped for.

Anon

May you have warmth in
your igloo, oil in your lamp
and peace in your heart.

Inuit proverb

God doesn't make the orange
juice. God makes the oranges.

Jesse Jackson

Thank God for dirty dishes; they have a tale to tell:
   while other folks go hungry, we're eating pretty well.
With home and health and happiness, we shouldn't want to fuss;
   for by this stack of evidence, God's very good to us.

Anon

A human being is a single being
– unique and unrepeatable.

Pope John Paul II

There are two ways to live your life. One
is as though nothing is a miracle. The
other is as though everything is a miracle.

Albert Einstein

May you live all the
days of your life.

Jonathan Swift

Reflect upon your present blessings, of which
every man has many – not on your past
misfortunes, of which all men have some.

Charles Dickens

There is nothing but God's grace.
We walk upon it.
We breathe it.
We live and die by it.

Robert Louis Stevenson

Normal day, let me be aware of the treasure
you are. Let me learn from you, love you, bless you
before you depart. Let me not pass you by in the quest of
some rare and perfect tomorrow. Let me hold you while I may,
for it may not always be so. One day I shall dig my nails into the
earth, or bury my face in the pillow, or stretch myself taut, or raise
my hands to the sky and want, more than all the world, your return.

Mary Jean Iron

Our Lord has written the promise of resurrection not in books alone, but in every leaf in springtime.

Martin Luther

There are two kinds of people: those who say to God, 'Thy will be done,' and those to whom God says, 'All right then, have it your way.'

C.S. Lewis

I am like a little pencil in God's hand. He does the writing. The pencil has nothing to do with it.

Mother Teresa

Live as if you like yourself, and it may happen.

Marge Piercy

Making the most of all you have

We have only this moment, sparkling like a star in our hand… and melting like a snowflake. Let us use it before it is too late.

Marie Beynon Ray

How far that little candle throws his beams! So shines a good deed in a naughty world.

William Shakespeare

Life is ten per cent what you make it, and ninety per cent how you take it.

Irving Berlin

I am dying, but otherwise I am quite well.

Edith Sitwell

'And did you get what you wanted from this life, even so?'
'I did.'
'And what did you want?'
'To call myself beloved, to feel myself beloved on the earth.'

Raymond Carver

All will be well, and every kind of thing will be well.

Julian of Norwich

A true friend is the best possession.

Anon

Wear a smile and have friends; wear a scowl and have wrinkles.

George Eliot

Life is not complex. We are complex. Life is simple, and the simple thing is the right thing.

Oscar Wilde

A hero is a man who does what he can.

Romain Rolland

Do not wish to be anything but what you are.

St Francis de Sales

Cooperation is doing with a smile what you have to do anyhow.

Anon

We should consider every
day lost on which we have
not danced at least once.

Friedrich Nietzsche

The butterfly counts not
months but moments, and
has time enough.

Rabindranath Tagore

The time is always right
to do what is right.

Martin Luther King, Jr

Years wrinkle the
face, but to give
up enthusiasm
wrinkles the soul.

Watterson Lowe

I have fought the good
fight, I have finished the
race, I have kept the faith.

Paul's second letter to Timothy

Just because a man lacks
the use of his eyes doesn't
mean he lacks vision.

Stevie Wonder

Don't hurry. Don't worry. You're
only here for a short visit – so be
sure to stop and smell the flowers.

Walter Hagen

Choose your rut carefully. You'll
be in it for the next ten miles.

Road sign in upstate New York

Actually, I'm an overnight success.
But it took twenty years.

Monty Hall

Bloom where you are planted.

Anon

*My mother said to me, 'If you become a
soldier, you'll be a general, if you become
a monk, you'll end up as the Pope.' Instead,
I became a painter and wound up as Picasso.*

Pablo Picasso

*What one has, one ought to
use; and whatever one does, one
should do with all one's might.*

Marcus Tullius Cicero

*I am not bound to win,
but I am bound to be true.
I am not bound to succeed,
but I am bound to live
up to what life I have.*

Abraham Lincoln

*Luck is everything... My good
luck in life was to be a really
frightened person. I'm fortunate
to be a coward, to have a low
threshold of fear, because a hero
couldn't make a good suspense film.*

Alfred Hitchcock

If we are facing in the
right direction, all we have
to do is keep on walking.

Buddhist proverb

To be content with what
we possess is the greatest
and most secure of riches.

Marcus Tullius Cicero

What you intuitively desire,
that is possible to you.

D.H. Lawrence

The miracle is not to fly in the air,
or to walk on the water,
but to walk on the earth.

Chinese proverb

If all our misfortunes were laid in one
common heap, whence everyone must
take an equal portion, most people would
be content to take their own and depart.

Socrates

While we live, let us live.

D.H. Lawrence

Work like you don't need the money,
   love like you've never been hurt,
dance like nobody's watching,
   sing like nobody's listening,
live like it's heaven on earth!

Anon

Some pursue
happiness, others
create it.

Anon

Working towards
a happier future

In the long run we shape our lives and
we shape ourselves. The process never
ends until we die, and the choices we
make are ultimately our own responsibility.

Eleanor Roosevelt

When I look at the
future, it's so bright,
it burns my eyes.

Oprah Winfrey

I am not afraid of storms, for I am learning how to sail my ship.

Louisa May Alcott

Nothing can bring you peace but yourself.

Ralph Waldo Emerson

What would life be if we had no courage to attempt anything?

Vincent van Gogh

Take risks. If you win, you'll be happy. If you lose, you'll be wise.

Anon

God is our refuge and strength, an ever present help in trouble. Therefore we will not fear.

Book of Psalms

As long as one keeps
searching, the
answers come.

Joan Baez

Destiny is not a matter
of chance, it is a matter
of choice; it is not a thing
to be waited for, it is a
thing to be achieved.

William J. Braun

Fear not that thy life
shall come to an end,
but rather that it shall
never have a beginning.

John Henry Newman

Just don't give up trying to do what you
really want to do. Where there are love and
inspiration, I don't think you can go wrong.

Ella Fitzgerald

To be what we are, and to
become what we are capable of
becoming, is the only end of life.

Robert Louis Stevenson

Grow old along
with me! The
best is yet to be.

Robert Browning

If you're not allowed to laugh in heaven, I don't want to go there.

Martin Luther

We must laugh before we are happy, for fear of dying without having laughed at all.

Jean de la Bruyere

Live as you will wish to have lived when you are dying.

Christian Furchtegott Gellert

Never give in! Never give in! In all things, great or small, large or petty, never give in except to convictions or honour and good sense!

Winston Churchill

It is sad to grow old, but nice to ripen.

Brigitte Bardot

It doesn't hurt to be optimistic. You can always cry later.

Lucimar Santos de Lima

But you're only human

Anyone can have an off decade.

Larry Co...

Oh, I am so
inadequate –
and I love myself!

Meg Ryan

I'm not overweight. I'm
just nine inches too short.

Shelley Winter...

It's OK if you mess
up. You should give
yourself a break.

Billy Joel

I can't say I was ever
lost, but I was bewildered
once for three days.

Daniel Boone

When in doubt, make a fool of yourself.
There is a microscopically thin line between
being brilliantly creative and acting like
the most gigantic idiot on earth.
    So what the hell – leap!

Cynthia Heimel

If you're going to be a failure, at
least be one at something you enjoy.

Sylvester Stallone

A good garden may
have some weeds.

Thomas Fuller

The essence of being
human is that one does
not seek perfection.

George Orwell

The first and great commandment
is don't let them scare you.

Elmer Davis

Think you can, think you
can't; either way, you'll be right.

Henry Ford

They were never defeated,
they were only killed.

Said of the French Foreign Legion

We can't all be heroes because
someone has to sit on the kerb
and clap as they go by.

Will Rogers

A man finds he has
been wrong at every
stage of his career,
only to deduce the
astonishing conclusion that
he is at last entirely right.

Robert Louis Stevenson

Life is not life unless
you make mistakes.

Joan Collins

In the game of life, nothing
is less important than
the score at half-time.

Anon

There ain't no cloud so thick that
the sun ain't shinin' on t'other side.

Rattlesnake

You don't get to choose how you're going to die. Or when.
You can only decide how you're going to live. Now.

Joan Baez

Don't curse the darkness.
Light a candle.

Chinese proverb

Advsersity is, to me at least,
a tonic and a bracer.

Sir Walter Scott

Here lies my past,
  goodbye I have kissed it;
thank you, kids,
  I wouldn't have missed it.

Ogden Nash

Everything is OK in the end.
If it's not OK, then it's not the end.

Anon

When we are not
sure, we are alive.

Graham Greene

After all, tomorrow
is another day.

Scarlett O'Hara

Always take an
emergency leisurely.

Chinese proverb

Green for growth and change

... when decisions and changes must be made to accept the past and find your future

If it is to be, it's up to me

Wasted time means wasted lives.

R. Shannon

Even if you're on the right track, you'll get run over if you just sit there.

Will Rogers

I wish I could stand on a busy corner, hat in hand, and beg people to throw me all their wasted hours.

Bernard Berenson

If you can't be a good example, then you'll just have to be a horrible warning.

Catherine Aird

And if not now, when?

The Talmud

This is not a dress rehearsal. This is it.

Tom Cunningham

Who is more foolish: the child afraid of the dark or the man afraid of the light?

Maurice Freehill

*None are so blind as
those who will not see.*

Anon

*Everybody thinks of changing humanity
and nobody thinks of changing himself.*

Leo Tolstoy

*There is in the worst of fortune the
best of chances for a happy change.*

Euripides

*Act like a doormat, and
people will walk on you.*

Anon

It's better to be a lion for a
day than a sheep all your life.

Sister Elizabeth Kenny

Those who have done nothing
but wait for their ship to come in
have already missed the boat.

Anon

For of all sad words of
tongues or pen, the
saddest are these
— it might have been.

John Greenleaf Whittier

You cannot run away
from a weakness.
You must sometimes fight
it out or perish; and if
that be so, why not now,
and where you stand?

Robert Louis Stevenson

One of these days
is none of these days.

H.G. Bohn

Happiness is a decision

I am the master of my fate;
I am the captain of my soul.

William Ernest Henley

When you have decided what
you believe, what you feel must
be done, have the courage to
stand alone and be counted.

Eleanor Roosevelt

Not to decide
is to decide.

Harvey Cox

My future is one I must make myself.

Louis l'Amour

The hour is ripe, and
yonder lies the way.

Virgil

*To know what you prefer, instead
of humbly saying 'Amen' to what
the world tells you you ought to
prefer, is to keep your soul alive.*

Robert Louis Stevenson

*If you think too long,
you think wrong.*

Jim Kaat

*How many cares one loses
when one decides not to be
something, but to be someone.*

Coco Chanel

'Mean to' don't pick no cotton.

Anon

Above all, try something.

Franklin Delano Roosevelt

We know what happens to people who stay in the middle of the road. They get run over.

Aneirin Bevan

Calculation never made a hero.

John Henry Newman

We have 40 million reasons for failure, but not a single excuse.

Rudyard Kipling

Depend on the rabbit's foot if you will, but it didn't work for the rabbit!

Anon

People who deliberate fully before they take a step will spend their lives on one leg.

Anthony de Mello

Seize the hour.

Sophocles

Moving on

Make voyages.
Attempt them.
There's nothing else.

Tennessee Williams

If there is no wind, row.

Latin proverb

The best way out of a problem is through it.

Anon

What we call failure
is not the falling down,
but the staying down.

Mary Pickford

Never mistake motion for action.

Ernest Hemingway

Plodding wins the race.

Aesop

I am not the smartest or most talented person in the world, but I succeeded because I keep going, and going, and going.

Sylvester Stallone

There is a time for departure even when there's no certain place to go.

Tennessee Williams

Behold the turtle. He makes progress only when he sticks his neck out.

James Bryant Conant

To achieve anything, you must be prepared to dabble on the boundary of disaster.

Stirling Moss

A journey of a thousand miles must begin with a single step.

Chinese proverb

It is never too late to be what you might have been.

George Eliot

It's the plugging away that
will win you the day,
so don't be a piker, old pard!
Just draw on your grit;
it's so easy to quit –
it's the keeping your chin
up that's hard.

Robert W. Service

Don't be afraid to take a big
step if one is indicated. You can't
cross a chasm in two small steps.

David Lloyd George

Turn your stumbling blocks
into stepping stones.

Anon

We all live under the
same sky, but we don't
all have the same horizon.

Konrad Adenauer

I'm a slow walker, but I never walk back.

Abraham Lincoln

Why should I
deem myself to
be a chisel, when
I could be the artist?

J.C.F. von Schiller

Whatever you can
do or dream you can,
begin it. Boldness has
genius, magic and power
in it. Begin it now.

Johann Wolfgang von Goethe

If your dreams are to come true, you must wake up

I want to do
it because I
want to do it.

Amelia Earhart

Man's reach should exceed his
grasp, or what's a heaven for?

Robert Browning

Here am I. Send me!

Book of Isaiah

I believe there's an inner power that makes winners or losers. And the winners are the ones who really listen to the truth of their hearts.

Sylvester Stallone

Yesterday I dared to struggle. Today I dare to win.

Bernadette Devlin

To do all that one is able to do is to be a man; to do all that one would like to do is to be a god.

Napoleon Bonaparte

There is just one life for each of us — our own.

Euripides

You have to take it as it happens, but you should try to make it happen the way you want to take it.

Old German proverb

The will of God will not take you where the grace of God cannot keep you.

Anon

Fortune sides with he who dares.

Virgil

*Every man is the
architect of his
own fortune.*

Sallust

*Try not to become a
man of success, but
rather a man of value.*

Albert Einstein

*I'll walk where my own nature
would be leading; it vexes
me to choose another guide.*

Emily Brontë

*We rate ability in people
by what they finish,
not by what they begin.*

Anon

*I won't give up, shut
up, let up or slow up.*

Robert Moorehead

*You go back to the
gym and you just
do it again and again
until you get it right.*

Arnold Schwarzenegger

Consequences
are what you get

If we can take the
worst, take the risk.

Dr Joyce Brothers

So often we try to alter circumstances to suit
ourselves, instead of letting them alter us.

Mother Maribel

If we cannot do what we will,
we must will what we can.

Yiddish proverb

When patterns are broken,
new worlds emerge.

Tuli Kupferberg

If you worry about what might
be, and wonder what might have
been, you will ignore what is.

Anon

The important thing is to learn
a lesson every time you lose.

John McEnroe

If we are intended for
great ends, we are
called to great hazards.

John Henry Newman

If you're not failing, you're
not trying anything.

Woody Allen

Some days you tame the tiger. And
some days the tiger has you for lunch.

Tug McGraw

The highest reward for a man's
toil is not what he gets for it,
but what he becomes by it.

John Ruskin

Make yourself indispensable,
and you'll be moved up.
Act as if you're indispensable,
and you'll be moved out.

Anon

Pain is inevitable.
Suffering is optional.

Anon

No guts, no glory.

Anon

The greatest discovery of
my generation is that man
can alter his life simply by
altering his attitude of mind.

William James

Not being beautiful was a true blessing – not being beautiful forced me to develop my inner resources. The pretty girl has a handicap to overcome.

Golda Meir

Hope hopes we have learned something from yesterday.

John Wayne

They can because they think they can.

Virgil

Do what you love. The money will flow.

Marsha Sinetar

Diamonds are only lumps of coal that stuck to their jobs.

B.C. Forbes

God helps them that help themselves.

Benjamin Franklin

Ask and it will be given to you; seek and you will find; knock and the door will be opened to you. For everyone who asks receives; he who seeks finds; and to him who knocks, the door will be opened.

Luke's Gospel

The prayer of the chicken hawk does not get him the chicken.

Swahili proverb

Set short-term goals and you'll win games. Set long-term goals and you'll win championships!

Anon

Success comes before work only in the dictionary.

Anon

We must act in spite of
fear – not because of it.

Anon

Putting up barriers

Circumstances – what are
circumstances? I make circumstances.

Napoleon Bonaparte

Some days the dragon wins.

Anon

If you don't like something
about yourself, change it. If
you can't change it, accept it.

Ted Shackelford

What counts is not
necessarily the size of the
dog in the fight, but the
size of the fight in the dog.

Dwight Eisenhower

If a plant's roots are too tight, repot.

**Headline from the gardening
section of The New York Times**

*Success is never found.
Failure is never fatal.
Courage is the only thing.*

Winston Churchill

*I'm in a wonderful position. I'm
unknown, I'm underrated, and
there's nowhere to go but up.*

Pierre S. DuPont IV

Little strokes fell great oaks.

Benjamin Franklin

The greater the difficulty, the
more glory in surmounting it.
Epicurus

A man would do nothing if he
waited until he could do it so
well that no one could find fault.
John Henry Newman

Adversity causes some
men to break, others
to break records.
William A. Ward

When you get to the end of your
rope, tie a knot and hang on.
Franklin Delano Roosevelt

You may have to fight
a battle more than
once to win it.
Margaret Thatcher

'Come to the edge,' he said.
They said, 'We are afraid.'
'Come to the edge,' he said.
They came.
He pushed them...
        and they flew.
Jonathan Livingstone Seagull

Nothing is particularly hard if
you divide it into small jobs.
Henry Ford

Text acknowledgments

Every effort has been made to trace and contact copyright owners for material used in this book. We apologise for any inadvertant omissions or errors.

pp. 12, 18: extracts by Dorothy Parker, copyright © The National Association for the Advancement of Colored People (NAACP) and the Estate of Dorothy Parker. Lion Publishing wish to thank the NAACP for authorising this use of Dorothy Parker's works.

p. 16: extract from 'Loss' by Wendy Cope, from *Serious Concerns* by Wendy Cope, published by Faber and Faber Ltd.

p. 25: extract from 'Friendship' by Elizabeth Jennings from *New Collected Poems*, published by Carcanet Press Ltd. Reproduced by permission of David Higham Associates Limited.

pp. 25 (John 15:13), 41 (Psalm 55:22), 49 (2 Chronicles 31:21): extracts from the Authorized Version of the Bible (The King James Bible), the rights in which are vested in the Crown, are reproduced by permission of the Crown's Patentee, Cambridge University Press.

p. 27: extract by Carol Van Klompenburg, from *Loving Your Preborn Baby*, copyright © 1990 Carol Van Klompenburg.

pp. 26, 27, 72: 'Family Court' by Ogden Nash, copyright © 1931 by Ogden Nash, renewed; 'The Parent' by Ogden Nash, copyright © 1933 by Ogden Nash, renewed; extract from 'Preface to the Past' by Ogden Nash, copyright © 1957 by Ogden Nash, renewed. All now copyright © Linell Nash Smith and Isabel Nash Eberstadt. Reprinted by permission of Curtis Brown, Ltd in the USA. Published by Andre Deutsch in the UK.

p. 30: 'The End': words and music by John Lennon and Paul McCartney. By kind permission of Northern Songs/Sony/ATV Music Publishing, copyright © 1969.

p. 36 (John 16:22): taken from the New Jerusalem Bible, published and copyright © 1985 by Darton, Longman and Todd Ltd and les Editions du Cerf, and by Doubleday, a division of Bantam Doubleday Dell Publishing Group, Inc. Used by permission of Darton, Longman and Todd Ltd, and Doubleday, a division of Random House, Inc.

pp. 37 (Isaiah 49:15–16), 55 (Psalm 118:24), 61 (2 Timothy 4:7), 66 (Psalm 46:1–2), 83 (Isaiah 6:8), 90 (Luke 11:9–10): scripture quotations taken from the *Holy Bible, New International Version*, copyright © 1973, 1978, 1984 by International Bible Society. Used by permission of Hodder & Stoughton Limited. All rights reserved. 'NIV' is a registered trademark of International Bible Society.

p. 38 (Mark 5:34): scriptures quoted from the Good News Bible published by The Bible Societies/HarperCollins Publishers Ltd, UK © American Bible Society 1966, 1971, 1976, 1992, used with permission.

p. 59: extract from 'Late Fragment' by Raymond Carver, from *A New Path to the Waterfall* by Raymond Carver, copyright © 1989 by the Estate of Raymond Carver. Used by permission of Grove/Atlantic Inc.